MW01155173

To ~~Barbara~~

Know your
Strength!

*"NEVER UNDERESTIMATE THE POWER
OF AFRICAN SPIRITUALITY"*

– Frantz Derenoncourt, Jr.

Based on a true story...

It was an extremely hot day on the British colony of Jamaica. Jamaica was previously a possession of Spain, but after a series of tricks, ruse, and furious fighting, Great Britain took control of the island from Spain in the year 1655. The British then authorized the kidnapping of hundreds of thousands of Africans and transported them to Jamaica to work as slaves on the many plantations to produce cash crops for sale.

On one of these plantations, an African man was working extremely hard to the point of exhaustion. Although the man was big and strong, the British slave masters forced him and all the other Africans to work from sun up to sun down. No breaks were allowed.

After a long hard day slaving on the plantation, the African man found peace and encouragement reading from his favorite book, The Holy Quran.
Knowing how to read and possessing books was strictly forbidden for the Africans on the plantation, so the African would have to be very careful that he would not get caught disobeying the laws because the punishment could mean his life. He often secretly taught his fellow Africans how to read and about spirituality.

The young man gained a reputation on the plantation for the vast knowledge he learned from his book. He became known as the "Book Man".

Although Boukman was one of the most productive Africans enslaved on the plantation, he was also known for being rebellious. He would often defy the slave masters' orders and stand up for the other Africans being mistreated. Usually the slave masters would not tolerate such disobedience from a slave but since Boukman was one of the biggest and strongest Africans on the plantation, his master decided to sell him to a different owner instead. The slave master knew that Boukman would demand a high price at auction.

The overseers arrested Boukman and put him on a boat to Saint Domingue, a French colony not too far away from Jamaica. Although there was nothing Boukman could do about his fate, he managed to get his book and hide it in his clothes. He would never see Jamaica again.

Once Boukman arrived in Saint Domingue, he was immediately led off of the boat and placed on an auction block where many French slave masters placed bids to buy him. All the potential buyers were impressed with his size and strength.

Just as his former British slave master thought, he sold for a premium price at auction.

Boukman was immediately put to work on the sugar plantation in the northern plains of Saint Domingue. At one point, the plantation commander noticed that he was hiding something in his pants. The commander ordered Boukman to hand over the book, but he refused. The book was the only possession he had and he did not want to part with it. The commander ordered Boukman to be disciplined for resisting an order. To teach him a lesson, the commander set the book on fire while still on Boukman's body leaving horrible burns and scars on his skin. The French slave master found this to be amusing.

Although Boukman was in physical pain, he was even more saddened and angry that his precious book was destroyed.

As the years went by, Boukman had grown to be well respected by everyone on the plantation. He was then given the job of slave driver. The slave driver, or commander, would be the person to discipline the enslaved Africans. Slave masters purposefully made Black people beat other Black people so they would resent each other and remain divided.

Boukman did not want the job, but the slave master threatened that he would be the one receiving the lashes if he refused.

Boukman unwillingly accepted his new position.

Boukman would often meet with his spiritual partner, Cecile Fatiman, for prayers and rituals. Cecile was a Mambo, Vodou priestess, and was also highly respected in the colony because of her strong beliefs and healing abilities. Cecile felt a great energy coming from Boukman and felt that he was the chosen one. Cecile had been planning a slave revolt for many years hoping to continue the legacy of the legendary maroon Makandal. Cecile would tell Boukman stories of Makandal's revolution and the struggle for freedom in Saint Domingue. They would secretly perform ceremonies together to gain strength and pay respect to their Ancestors.

Boukman became a Hougan, Vodou priest. Vodou is a spiritual practice inherited from his ancestors in West Africa.

After many years as slave driver, Boukman's master promoted him to be his coach driver. The coachman drives the slave master to wherever he wants to go.

The year is now 1791, and many events were taking place all around the colony and back in the mother country, France. The French Revolution was in full swing and the news had spread to Saint-Domingue. The poor French people wanted equal rights for all and were willing to fight for it. Althoughthe French Revolution would not have freed the enslaved Africans,rumors spread like wildfire that the King of France, Louis XVI, wouldgive them an extra free day. Boukman and many other enslaved Africans believed that the moment was ripe for them to take action for their own freedom.

Boukman and Cecile Fatiman decided to recruit all of the influential African leaders from plantations across the North of the colony to meet to discuss the important move. It was Cecile's job to go from plantation to plantation in the middle of the night to give the details of when and where the meeting would be held. She would sometimes travel miles in one night on recruiting trips.

It was a risky and difficult task, but she knew the importance of her mission.

On the full moonlit night of August 14, 1791... Boukman and Cecile Fatiman directed a revolutionary meeting in the thickly wooded Bwa Kayiman area. Two delegates from every plantation across the North attended the meeting. Over two hundred frightful yet daring Africans were present.

The purpose of the meeting was to put the finishing touch on the slave revolt they had been planning for a long time. Many of the delegates wanted to start the revolution that very night but the final decision was made to wait until the following week.

At the conclusion of the meeting, Boukman and Cecile Fatiman performed a Vodou ceremony. Before Europeans introduced their version of Christianity to Africa, Vodou was the means by which many Africans spiritually communicated with their powerful ancestors as well as the forces of Nature. The enslaved Africans prayed for strength and guidance as they set forth on this fateful journey to freedom. Everyone in attendance took an oath of secrecy and solidarity. Boukman preached a powerful prayer, which would go down in history.

On August 22, 1791, the enslaved Africans began to revolt against their masters all over the North of Saint-Domingue. They went from plantation to plantation, burning crops, houses, sugar refineries, and everything else down to the ground.

With the spirit of their ancestors with them, the Africans were fearless in their fighting. Boukman led a formidable army of enslaved Africans as well as maroons. Some estimated Boukman to be at the head of more than 15,000 men and women during the early months of the revolution.

Most of the rebels in Boukman's army did not have guns. The rebels used whatever they could get their hands on as weapons: fire, stones, sticks, wood, etc. They mostly used farming equipment such as machetes, which were used to cut down sugar cane on the plantations. Even though the Africans held an advantage in numbers, the French troops were professionally trained, highly equipped, and disciplined when it came to the art of battle.

The rebels did not have advanced weapons like the French military but they used knowledge of the land and their surroundings to gain the upper hand during many battles. They would use sneak attacks, nighttime raids, and would often ambush the French troops when they were least expecting it.

The African rebels' guerilla warfare tactics inflicted heavy losses on the French forces.

In November 1791, Boukman made a bold attempt to attack the capital city of Saint-Domingue, Cap-Francais. During the attempt, he was captured by the French military who rushed to have him executed and presented as an example to the rebelling Africans.

Now that the leader of the rebels was gone, the French slave masters thought that would eliminate the revolt and force all the Africans to return to the plantations as slaves, never to rise up again. They were wrong.

The person that would eventually take over the leadership of the rebel army and lead the enslaved Africans to many victories over their European enemies became one of the most brilliant military generals in history. He trained and structured the African rebels into a highly organized and disciplined military force. It soon gained the reputation of being one of the most feared armies in the entire world.

He started off as the one who took care of the horses, then rose to become the rebel army's medicine man. First known in Saint Domingue as Francois Dominique Breda, as he gained greater knowledge of himself and his mission he would eventually go down in history as the great Toussaint Louverture.

Boukman did not survive to see the completion of the revolution he helped begin in Saint Domingue. However, the African rebels were eventually successful in driving the French slave masters out of the colony and creating the first free black nation in the Americas.

Many Africans believed that after they died their spirits go back to their homeland of Africa.
Boukman has taken his place among his powerful ancestors from the Kingdom of Dahomey who also sacrificed their lives fighting colonists for the well being of their African brothers and sisters.

Boukman has cemented his legacy as a fearless fighter, a spiritual leader, and one of the greatest heroes in history.

GLOSSARY

Vodou – A religion and spiritual discipline practiced mostly by people of African descent as a way to connect with ancestors, angels, plants, and animals.

Hougan – A vodou priest. A man who is knowledgeable about vodou and leads vodou ceremonies.

Mambo – A vodou priestess. A woman who is knowledgeable about vodou and leads vodou ceremonies.

Colony – a country or area under the full political and/or military control of another country and occupied by settlers from that country.

Slave – A person who is the legal property of another and is forced to obey them.

Plantation – An estate on which crops such as sugar, coffee, and tobacco are cultivated by resident labor.

Slave Master – A person who has slaves working for them.

Revolution – A forcible overthrow of a government or social order in favor of a new system.

Auction Block – A platform from which people were sold as slaves to the highest bidder.

Overseer – A person who supervises others and makes sure slaves are constantly working.

Guerilla warfare – A form of irregular warfare in which a small group of fighters use military tactics including ambushes, sabotage, raids, hit and run tactics, and mobility to fight a larger, less mobile, and more traditional military.

Maroon – A fugitive slave who often settles in inaccessible, mountainous areas.

Slave revolt – An armed uprising of slaves or oppressed people.

Rebel – A person who rises in opposition or armed resistance against an established government or ruler.

The Holy Quran – The central religious text of Islam, which Muslims believe to be a revelation from God (Allah)

Bwa Kayiman/Bois Caiman – The site of the vodou ceremony during which the first major slave insurrection of the Haitian Revolution was planned.

Kingdom of Dahomey – An African kingdom (located within the area of the present-day country of Benin) that existed from about 1600 until 1894. Also well known for the Dahomey Amazons, a corps of female soldiers.

Saint Domingue – Colonial name for Haiti between 1697 until 1804.

Cap-Francais – The capital of Saint Domingue/Haiti until the 19th century.

Cash Crop – A crop produced for its commercial value rather than for use by the grower.

French Revolution – An uprising in France against the monarchy from 1789 to 1799 which resulted in the establishment of France as a republic.

Boukman's Prayer

"The God who created the earth, who created the sun that gives us light.

The God who holds up the ocean, who makes the thunder roar.

Our God who has ears to hear, You who are hidden in the clouds, who watch us from where you are.

You see all that the white has made us suffer. The white man's god asks him to commit crimes.

But the God within us wants to do good.

Our God, who is so good, so just, He orders us to avenge our wrongs.

It's He who will direct our arms and bring us the victory.

It's He who will assist us.

Throw away the image of the white man's god who is so pitiless, and listen to the voice of liberty that sings in all our hearts.

BIO

Frantz Derenoncourt, Jr. is a first generation Haitian-American born and raised in East Flatbush, Brooklyn, NY. As a child growing up in Brooklyn in the early 80s, Frantz was often picked on for being Haitian. Teachers could never pronounce his name correctly and the students would always have a cruel Haitian joke on hand. At times, he felt ashamed to be Haitian until he started reading about Haitian history. The fact that his little country accomplished something that no other nation had accomplished gave him a tremendous sense of pride. He started reading everything he could get his hands on in regards to the Haitian Revolution and retelling the stories to his children, Chase and Maven. When he saw that his kids were just as excited as he was, Frantz then realized that this fascinating story needs to be told in a way that even a 1st grade reader can appreciate the accomplishment of his ancestors. Thus, *Haiti: The First Black Republic* was born followed by *Makandal: The Black Messiah* and *Boukman: Black Revolution.*

Get the whole collection
at
www.thorobredbooks.com